MESSER MAGAZIN WORKSHOP

Ernst G. Siebeneicher-Hellwig and Jürgen Rosinski

Forging Japanese Knives
For Beginners

From steel production to the
finished tanto and hocho
with practical wire binding

4880 Lower Valley Road • Atglen, PA 19310

Published by Schiffer Publishing, Ltd.
4880 Lower Valley Road
Atglen, PA 19310
Phone: (610) 593-1777; Fax: (610) 593-2002
E-mail: Info@schifferbooks.com

For our complete selection of fine books on this and related subjects, please visit our website at www.schifferbooks.com. You may also write for a free catalog.

This book may be purchased from the publisher. Please try your bookstore first.

We are always looking for people to write books on new and related subjects. If you have an idea for a book, please contact us at proposals@schifferbooks.com.

Schiffer Publishing's titles are available at special discounts for bulk purchases for sales promotions or premiums. Special editions, including personalized covers, corporate imprints, and excerpts can be created in large quantities for special needs. For more information, contact the publisher.

CONTENTS

FOREWORD

With this book I have fulfilled a dream I've had for a long time: to completely construct a Japanese knife from the very first work step to the final touches. Starting with the search for iron ore to the smelting of steel in the bloomery furnace, it includes the forging of the blade, the partial hardening of the blade edge, and continues to assembling the knife.

I believe this dream is also shared by other knife enthusiasts. And I hope this book will help them to realize their dreams as well.

With respect to forging and welding the blade steel, we follow our two books *Basic Knife Making*" and *Forging Damascus Steel Knives For Beginners*. We start with a bloomery furnace, then craft a Japanese kitchen knife and tanto blade from the produced steel. Actually our bloomery furnace is a Celtic one. However, with respect to technology, there is no difference between a Japanese and a Celtic bloomery. But since we are living in the heartland of the Celts, it was obvious to erect a Celtic furnace here.

I hope this book finds as positive a resonance as both previous books have and encourages our readers to continue with the beautiful hobby of knifemaking – or to start it.

Ernst G. Siebeneicher-Hellwig

First of all, thanks to all those who helped in the making of this book with words and deeds, above all to our friend Noriaki Narushima, who, in his friendly and humble manner, brought much of the Japanese culture to our attention and also showed us the limits of what is possible. Our thanks also go to Andreas Schweikert, who allowed me to look over his shoulder during one of his bloomery projects and gave me the chance to learn a lot.

With writing this book a dream has come true which I had since childhood, because I have always been fascinated by the Asian culture of martial arts and its weapons. When I started with martial arts in 1978, the possession of a Japanese sword was for me like reaching the goal of life. Lacking the chance to buy such a sword, I started with forging a sword blade from simple tool steel during my second year of apprenticeship. Looking back with today's knowledge, this was a very amateurish project, but back then I was a happy little samurai.

In Japan there is a proverb: the more a rice ear ripens, the deeper its head sinks. Translated freely, for me this means: the greater the knowledge, the more humble and modest your attitude ought to be. Thus, I first want to bow to the old masters and their art, because I was able to take a glimpse of their forging skills by means of my own work.

I also bow to the readers who have the courage to rely on the findings of our work during the production of their own steel. And thus I finally may be allowed to wish that everybody who wants to produce their own steel will have a similar success and as much fun during work as we had.

Jürgen Rosinski

Important Tip:
Prior to starting your work, please read the
safety recommendations in the appendix!

A FEW WORDS
UP FRONT

Forging as a hobby has been booming in recent years. More and more people are discovering how much joy it can be to shape a piece of steel with fire and hammer – an archaic craft, which, especially in our time, radiates a lot of fascination.

It is even more fascinating also to create the steel with which to forge a knife for yourself. In this volume the entire process is shown: from searching for the iron ore to building and using a bloomery furnace, up to forging, sharpening and mounting a knife.

Actually, two knives are described here – a Japanese hocho (kitchen knife) and a tanto, the short weapon of a samurai. This volume shows a great variety of topics and work steps in compact form. Forging isn't shown in great detail here. Whoever hasn't forged any blade themselves yet, thus ought to take a look at *Basic Knife Making: From Raw Steel to a Finished Stub Tang Knife* by the same authors.

This is the latest volume in a workshop series that assembles a multitude of themes all around knifemaking in a way which enables you not only to follow each step but to do it yourself, too. We emphasize especially the usability of all the volumes in practice and workshop.

Thus all the volumes are provided with a wire binding (more specifically: with a so-called Wire-O binding). This way, the book stays open when you put it down. Also, we took care that the size of images and fonts is big enough to still be recognizable and readable when the book is lying next to you during work.

We have tried to explain every step of work in the most comprehensive way. But before you pick up your tools, you nevertheless ought to completely read all the descriptions and explanations in this book. This way, you'll know what to expect and won't be confronted with unpleasant surprises later on.

I wish you much fun and success with your work!

Hans Joachim Wieland

Chief Editor, Messer Magazin

INTRODUCTION

In this book we will show how – starting with ore and charcoal – steel is produced in the bloomery furnace, how blade blanks are forged from this, and how these blades are made ready for use. Then we show you how a hocho, a Japanese kitchen knife, is made from one of these forged blades. Besides this, we forge a tanto blade, which is of technically different construction. For those readers who can't or don't want to follow the entire way from ore to the finished knife, we also show how a newcomer can construct a knife from bought materials.

Raw material:
a lump of bog iron ore.

This can be made from it: a forged hocho blade.

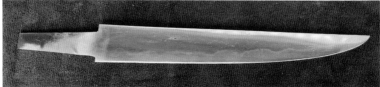

Same material but different construction: a tanto blade.

In this book, we describe the construction and use of a bloomery furnace similar to those already used by Celts and Romans, which were in use up to the Middle Ages. The variant we used is different only with respect to employing a motor and electric current to provide fresh air instead of relying on muscular strength and a bellows. We also used bricks and chamotte cement for erecting the furnace.

First of all, we want to talk a bit about the historical roots of the bloomery process in Europe. Then we describe the production of knives in Japanese style. This apparent inconsistency is not a real one because the European bloomery process is based on the same principle as the Japanese one (tatara).

1.1 History

The Celts were the first to successfully practice iron production and processing in Central Europe. For the production of iron they used so-called bloomery furnaces, also called Renn furnaces. The expression Renn furnace is derived from the German verb "rinnen" (to run, to flow; the slag flows out of the furnace after tapping).

In order to produce iron from the ores found in nature (iron oxides), the iron has to be separated from the oxygen. This process is called reduction. Here, the chemical bonds between iron and oxygen are separated. For this separation, as with all chemical processes of this type, it is necessary to supply energy. Since the energy demand for this process is quite high, iron can't be simply smelted at the campfire. For this task you need a furnace which is able to produce the required heat of more than 1000°C.

It is puzzling why the early metallurgists, as early as the late Neolithic Age, built furnaces and heated stones whose appearance gave no clue to their containing metal to such an extent that, when hot, the chemically bound copper was set free and dripped from the stones.

One explanation takes a detour via pottery: humans discovered early on that loam or clay, from which they made their receptacles, becomes hard under the influence of heat and thus also becomes more useful than air-dried wares. This discovery might have been made during a

Early inventors:
Celtic family (figures in the
Huttermuseum, at Erdweg in
Upper Bavaria, Germany).

Primordinal steel production:
a bloomery furnace in the
Archaeology Park Altmühltal, built
and operated by Jürgen Rosinski.

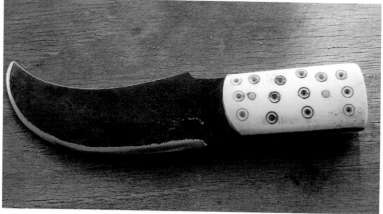

Tool and weapon: reconstruction of a Celtic knife from
Riedenburg-Untereggersberg near Kelheim, Germany.

fire which broke out in a wooden hut, or when some Stone Age people heated up food in clay vessels at the campfire and thereby inadvertently created the first ceramic receptacles. The step towards ceramics can be explained logically.

But what moved prehistoric humans to heat up stones without any obvious benefit and accidentally discover their inner values in the form of metal? Stone Age people, too, loved pretty things: they created jewelry, painted cave walls, and decorated their ceramic vessels. It is possible that our ancestors wanted to decorate some of the vessels with colors and also used milled, colorful, stone powder for this task. While using malachite, which was loved because of its green color, the copper contained in the stone could have been smelted and thus become apparent. This surprising result might have moved the first experimenters to also check other stones for inner values by heating them.

The fact is that humans, after smelting copper, alloyed tin with copper during the Bronze Age and thus created bronze – a metal which gave its name to an entire era. During this epoch, important inventions and discoveries were made and the foundation was laid for our civilization. We should not forget that the Egyptian pyramids were built during the Bronze Age. At this time, iron was only known in the form of mete-

Valuable back then: original socketed axe and reconstruction of a knife from the bronze age.

Evidence of the past: a Celtic burial mound from about 500 B.C. near Scheyern, Germany.

oric iron, which was often said to have magical properties because of its "heavenly origin" and because it was seen as a gift of the gods.

Iron in its originally known form was unusable for tools. It took many centuries until the next step in the production of metal was made and the process for the creation of iron suited for tools was discovered. For the production of iron, much hotter furnaces were necessary than those that were used for the creation of bronze.

The invention of the bloomery furnace was the decisive step for the production of useful iron. In Anatolia, the Indo-Germanic people of the Hittites managed to produce iron tools already around 1500 B.C. In Northern Europe, the Iron Age began as late as circa 800 B.C., starting with the Celtic Hallstatt culture.

1.2 Basics

First, we want to clarify the difference between iron and steel. This is simple: steel is forgeable iron which contains at least 0.1 percent of carbon. The natural upper limit for the carbon content is about two percent. Above this, steel is no longer forgeable; it is then called cast iron. Only modern steel types which are produced in a powder-metallurgical way can contain more carbon. The hardening of steel is a function of its carbon content. During hardening, the steel is heated up to the appropriate temperature and then quenched (usually in water or oil). By this method – to put it simply – an inner warping of the steel matrix is created, which provides a substantially higher stability and toughness.

As mentioned before, pure iron in nature can only be found as iron meteorites. Apart from this, it is usually bound to oxygen as iron oxide. To free the iron from its bond with oxygen, the ore has to be reduced. This means, the oxygen is separated from the iron by supplying energy (i.e. at high temperature). Iron has the relatively high melting point of 1535°C. But iron compounds can already be reduced to iron at around 1100°C without it becoming fluid. This was done in bloomery furnaces for many centuries.

Traditional bloomery furnaces were fueled with charcoal. It contains carbon (C). Iron ore contains iron in connection with oxygen (FeO). When the coal is burnt, carbon dioxide is created (CO_2). With the re-

"Heavenly" origin: pendant of meteoric iron and part of a meteorite already prepared for subsequent processing as material for knife bolsters.

duced oxygen supply in the bloomery furnace there is not enough oxygen to create carbon dioxide.

Instead carbon monoxide (CO) is produced. This carbon monoxide searches for more oxygen to form carbon dioxide. Iron ore contains the needed oxygen. The carbon monoxide joins with the oxygen (O) of the iron ore (FeO) to create carbon dioxide. Iron (Fe) is left over. The process of rusting, i.e. the oxidation (the bonding of Fe and O to form FeO), is reversed by this reduction.

The process can be visualized as the carbon monoxide streaming around the glowing ore. After the carbon monoxide has virtually sucked up the oxygen contained in the iron ore, the iron forms a viscous slurry with lots of slag. This way a sponge-like structure is created, the so-called bloom or loop.

1.3 The Iron Ore

Depending on their origin and composition, several types of iron ore are distinguished. Close to the Austrian town Eisenerz iron ore (siderite) with an average iron content of 33 percent is still mined from open pits at the Erzberg. From the Roman province Noricum, in what is the state of Carinthia (Kärnten) today, came the famous Ferrum Noricum, a steel type of high quality from which weapons were made for the Roman legions.

Bog Iron Ore

Bog iron ore is naturally found in iron-containing soils within swampy areas, quite often at shallow depths. Bog iron ore is created when iron-containing water reacts with soil deposits. The metal proportion varies widely but can be as much as 45 percent. Bog iron ore can be recognized by its reddish brown color.

Bean Ore

Bean Ore or limonite (brown hematite) is named after its bean-like shape. Among other places, it can be found in the Swabian and Frankonian Jura of Germany. It is created of limestone and iron dissolved in water.

Ironsand

In Japan iron is produced from very pure ironsand. Its iron content is very high and the sand has only a very small content of unwanted ingredients such as sulfur and phosphorus. Ironsand is also the raw material used for the production of traditional samurai swords. But even in Germany there exist deposits of ironsand. Unfortunately, the ore is practically not available for purchase. Thus the only thing left

Can be recognized by its red color: bog iron ore.

In the typical shape which reminds one of beans: bean ore:

Ore from an old Celtic funnel-shaped mine shaft close to the Celtic Oppidum Alkimoennis near Kelheim.

Eponym: Iron ore from the Austrian town Eisenerz ("iron ore").

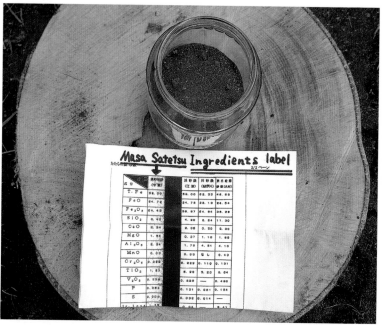

Very pure and sought after: Japanese ironsand.

is to search for it yourself. This also has its special appeal: to forge a knife for which you not only made the steel yourself but have found the ore for doing so as well is the optimum for the true enthusiast. Besides this, it is not as difficult as it looks.

Deposits of bog iron ore are widespread in Germany. An ore deposit, for example, is close to Tittling in the Frankonian Jura. One district of Tittling bears the field name "Erzwäsche" (ore cleaning). We visited this place as part of our project, especially since we had received tips that, besides bean ore, the desired ironsand could be found there as well.

After a short search we discovered it: in dried-out springs in a forest behind the village. This type of spring, in German called "Kopfquelle", constitutes a small crater in the ground from which water wells up after rainfalls. The water carries material from beneath the surface along with it. In our case the soil at the bottom of the spring was mixed with a considerable amount of ironsand.

Part of a meadow with a so-called "Kopfquelle". You can easily spot the crater in the meadow ground on the picture.

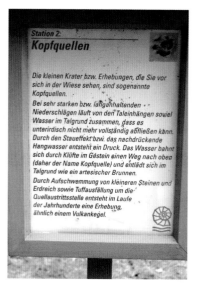

Informative: a sign close to the town Tittling in the Frankonian Jura of Germany.

With a magnet at the hammer: the sand is checked for iron-containing grains.

There is indeed iron in there, as the magnet proves: a bucket filled with soil which is mixed with ironsand.

With a magnet attached to a stick or simply stuck to a hammer, the sand at the bottom of the well can be checked. The iron ore sticks to the magnet. Material containing iron is about twice as heavy as simple rocks. In addition, red color is always a hint that iron may be found in the soil or rocks.

1.4 The Furnace

With respect to the technical processes, our bloomery project corresponds to the old methods and is based on experimental archaeology. But we consciously did not conduct experimental archaeology up to the tiniest detail. So we abstained from producing the charcoal ourselves and from installing air supply systems driven by human muscle force. We also didn't dress as Celts or Germanic people and forewent uttering magic formulas. As fuel we used charcoal, as in ancient times – but the type used for grilling from the DIY store plus a few dry logs to start the fire.

With respect to building the furnace we proceeded in such a way that it can be rebuilt and used in practice with as little effort as possible. The old Celts and Germanic people didn't build their furnaces with bricks. And of course, water hoses weren't used for air supply and vacuum cleaner motors were unknown as well. The critical purists among our readers may forgive us, but to erect and use the bloomery furnace within acceptable time we had to abstain from maximum authenticity. I think the practitioners will be grateful for this.

Our aim was to show how it works to produce a useful blade from a proverbial handful of dirt and to design and describe the worksteps so that they are comprehensible and reproducible. We configured the book in a way that the reader can also execute individual worksteps of the project only.

The following photos were taken during a bloomery project in the company Dictum's course program.

MATERIAL FOR THE BLOOMERY FURNACE

Fired bricks (for example from a demolished building)
Clay (from a field)
Quartz sand (DIY store)
Chamotte cement (DIY store)
Ceramic pipes (spacer tubes) (specialized shops for pottery needs)
Air tube (water tube) (DIY store)
Blower (old vacuum cleaner motor)

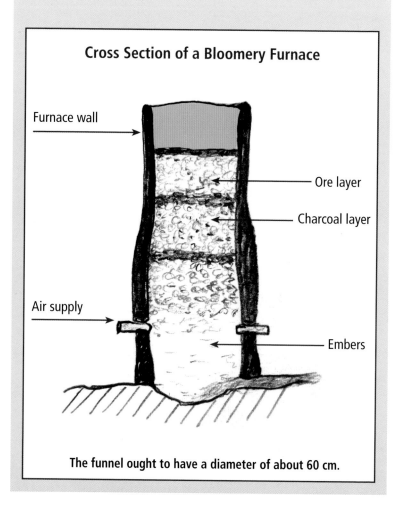

Cross Section of a Bloomery Furnace

Furnace wall

Ore layer

Charcoal layer

Air supply

Embers

The funnel ought to have a diameter of about 60 cm.

CONSTRUCTION OF THE BLOOMERY

For our bloomery project we chose a paved ground-level surface. This is not authentic, but very practical because no large damage to the ground has to be repaired after taking down the furnace. The base is made from sand. The layer of sand is used as a foundation and eases cleaning up after taking apart the furnace.

We start with sand on the paved ground.

At first, the sand is leveled.

High-fired solid bricks serve as the ground of the bloomery furnace.

To save time, we used old bricks from a demolished building for this project. The small, handy bricks simplify the dismantling. In early days a meshwork of willow twigs, which was coated with clay, was used for building the furnace. We used heat-resistant chamotte cement. To prevent the clay used for coating from becoming too fat we made it a bit lean by mixing in sand. In order to supply the furnace with oxygen from the air, two ceramic pipes are walled in at the side.

The bricks for the walls are being prepared.

The first row is put down.

The clay is mixed with sand and thus becomes lean.

The wall is constructed row after row.

The ceramic pipes for venting are placed at the sides.

The bottom of the furnace is covered with clay.

The wall is covered with clay on its outside.

The inside is covered thickly with clay as well.

Not beautiful, but functional: the furnace is finished.

As a source for fresh air we used old vacuum cleaner motors. The air was led with a hose to the old water tubes. The tubes were stuck into the ceramic ducts. The air was blown into the furnace by two ducts. To connect the exhaust port of the motor with the water tube, a piece of bicycle tube held by hose fittings does the trick. The completed furnace is filled up with logs and heated up for the first time in order to dry it.

Covered with clay:
view of the inside.

Air hose and blower are attached.

The furnace is heated up for drying.

OPERATING THE BLOOMERY

For operating the bloomery furnace the charcoal is mashed in order to achieve better combustion and greater heat. The ore as well is broken up prior to smelting to provide a large surface for reduction. After breaking, it is first roasted on a suitable grid over the campfire for several hours.

The ore is mixed with lime in equal parts. The lime causes the phosphorus, an unwanted companion to the iron, to be bound to the slag during the process. To this you can add hammer scale. Hammer scale is created as cinder during forging and is a compound of oxygen and iron.

The furnace is filled with logs and lit. Then charcoal and ore are stacked in alternate layers. If the air hose is removed, you can glimpse through the tube every once in a while and see the embers. You can also determine by the noise of the furnace whether it burns well. During a good process the furnace hisses and bubbles when fluid slag has already formed. You can take a sample with the help of a steel rod. If the sample is magnetic, the reduction process is proceeding well.

After about ten hours the furnace is taken down in order to retrieve the bloom. The bloom is a sponge-like mixture of iron, slag and charcoal remains. It is the result of the entire effort.

MATERIAL FOR THE BLOOMERY'S OPERATION
- iron ore (material procurement see chapter 1.3)
- logs
- charcoal for grilling (DIY store)
- lime (store for construction materials)

The charcoal is mashed.
This way you can achieve greater heat in the furnace.

The furnace is lit.

At the beginning there is still lots of smoke.

After it is heated up, the furnace is filled with iron ore from the top.

The mixture of ore and lime on the glowing charcoal.

In between, the charcoal is replenished several times.

A look through the air tube shows the bright, hot embers.

We take a sample with a rod of mild steel.

The sample is magnetic – a good sign.

For the described bloomery project 160 kilograms of charcoal and 45 kilograms of iron ore were used. The result was a bloom with a weight of 8.8 kilograms. The authors successfully completed several bloomery projects. In the Archaeology Park Altmühltal in Neueissing, Germany, a Celtic forge with bloomery furnace was rebuilt at a historical place in the Altmühl valley near Kelheim. At this place bloomery projects under the leadership of Jürgen Rosinski are still taking place.

It served its purpose: the furnace is torn down.
It can't be used more than once.

Precious sediments: the glowing bloom becomes visible.

The result of the strenuous work: the bloom after its recovery.

Some small pieces of steel out of the furnace.

Below is a part of the loop, cut apart and polished.

In the close-up view the sponge structure of the bloom is distinctly visible.

THE EASY WAY

Whoever wants to start directly with steel from the furnace without going through the laborious bloomery process beforehand can purchase true Japanese tamahagane in specialized shops – at least it is offered there every now and then. Tamahagane is steel which is smelted from very pure ironsand in special furnaces. The process is very similar to the European bloomery process. Tamahagane is the traditional raw material for Japanese swords.

With some luck, it is available commercially: tamahagane from Japan.

FROM BLOOM TO BILLET

We couldn't forge a blade straight from our bloom. The raw material has to be treated further in order to achieve the necessary structure and purity.

4.1 Determining the Carbon Content

Carbon plays a decisive role within the steel. From about 0.2 percent of carbon onwards steel becomes hardenable. Only then is it suitable for tool blades. Above roughly two percent of carbon content steel is no longer forgeable and is called cast iron.

With increasing carbon content steel gains more hardness but also loses toughness. This fact is decisive in the production of knives. If the steel is too hard it breaks under load and thus is not suitable for knives or swords.

In practice, the good qualities of a very hard steel type, especially its high edge retention, can be combined with the flexibility of soft steel by welding together two different steel types. Japanese bladesmiths thus combine soft cores with hard edges. This connection is flexible but nevertheless has a hard blade edge – ideal for a sword or knife.

To use the qualities of the different steel types you first have to know whether the steel in question has a high or low carbon content. In the following we will show how the steel can be judged correctly with respect to its carbon content.

By means of the so-called spark testing, the method normally used, you can easily and reliably find out whether the carbon content of a steel type is high or low. For this the steel is pressed against the running wheel of a bench grinder or the belt of a belt grinder. For steel with high carbon content, spark testing shows a large number of star-shaped carbon explosions among the sparks.

Spark testing at low carbon content: only few "stars" are visible.

Spark testing at high carbon content: the many star-shaped explosions can be recognized easily.

In the bloomery furnace metal with varying carbon content is created, controlled by influences such as the temperature and proportions of carbon and oxygen within the hot gases. Knowing that the distribution of carbon within the loop can be quite irregular, you can choose between two ways for further processing: taking the loop as it is and distributing the carbon evenly by folding and welding the billet many times. This way we followed for the production of our tanto blade.

The second method is to check individual parts for their carbon content, to sort them and to use them purposefully wherever the special qualities of the individual steel types are needed: soft steel at the sides of the blade and its back, hard steel at the blade's edge.

4.2 Forging

As we saw on the first images of our bloom, it is rather a sponge than a solid piece of metal. In addition, this sponge is interspersed with residues of slag und unburnt charcoal. By forging out and folding for several times the piece becomes more compact, flaws are welded shut and impurities are removed. Besides this, a homogeneous distribution of the carbon is achieved within the forged piece.

To forge the steel it first has to be cut into handy pieces. For better handling during forging, a rod from mild steel is welded to the bloom.

Prior to forging, flux (borax) should be strewn on the bloom. This aid prevents further creation of oxides and supports the forging process. In former times, fine quartz sand (pit-iron sand) was used. The sand or borax melts in the heat and prevents oxygen from the surrounding air from reacting with the iron and creating unwanted oxides. This makes for good weldings.

Forge welding is the joining of steels into a permanent compound under high heat. The pieces to be welded need to have shiny surfaces without dirt on the sides where they are welded together. Prior to welding existing scale is removed with a wire brush or file, then flux is strewn on.

The bloom is cut into handy pieces with the angle grinder.

The bloom with handle in front of the forging fire.

Flux is strewn onto the bloom.

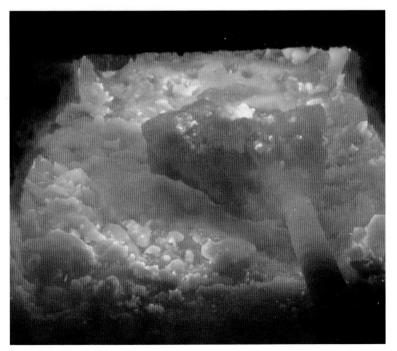

The bloom in the fire.

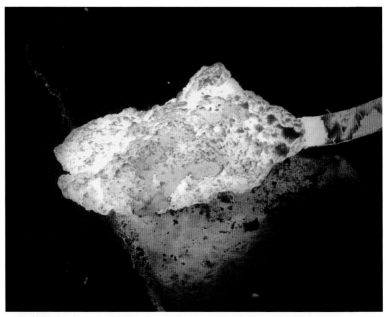

With a forged-on rod for better handling: the bloom on the anvil.

The billet is created: the bloom is forged flat.

The temperature is about 1,200 to 1,300°C. The heat color is lemon yellow. After the forging temperature has been reached, the parts are welded together on the anvil with moderate hammer blows. In a professional workshop the spring hammer is used for this. In the hobbyist's workshop manual work on the anvil is the answer. The billet is beaten out to increase its length, folded, welded and beaten out again several times.

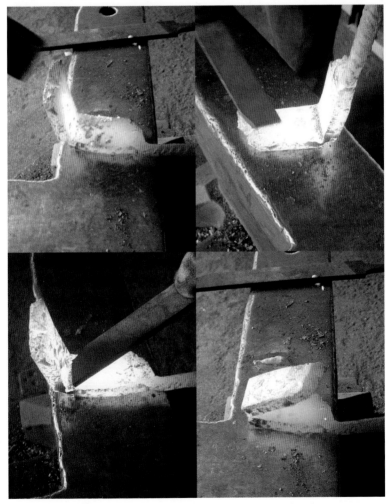

For folding, the billet receives a notch in the center and is then bent as shown.

The first folding process is finished.

The folded billet is heated up to forging temperature and forge-welded.

After this, the billet (here shown already finished) is forged out lengthwise and folded again.

For further treatment the billet is ground to a rectangular cross section. After grinding, you can see whether the billet has visible flaws or not.

If flaws are detected, the billet is forged some more.

The billet is ground at the belt grinder.

Not yet satisfying: a piece with distinctly visible flaws.

TANTO – THE JAPANESE DAGGER

5.1 Basics

Before we start to make our tanto, here a brief overview of the most common Japanese knives.

Katana (long sword)

The katana was the main weapon of the samurai. Swords of famous smiths were said to have magical properties. The samurai believed that their soul lived within the katana. Thus the cleaning of the sword was seen as purging their soul.

Japanese smiths in traditional clothes shown while forging a sword blade.

Wakizashi (short sword, blade length 40 to 51 cm)

The short sword was a replacement in case the katana broke in combat. It was used as a weapon inside buildings, for hara-kiri (seppuku) or for cutting off the head of killed enemies.

Tanto (dagger, blade length 28 to 40 cm)

The tanto was used as a battle knife, usually in close combat. Besides the wakizashi, it was also used for ritualistic suicide.

Aikuchi (dagger)

A tanto with a small guard.

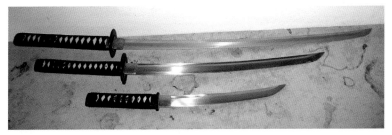

Classical triplet: katana, wakizashi and tanto.

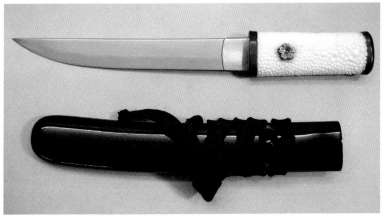

Aikuchi: a dagger without any guard (tsuba) or with only a small tsuba.

There are different types with respect to the construction of Japanese blades. Here are the most important ones:

Maru kitae: carbon steel and soft iron mixed. Such a blade basically has uniform elasticity and hardness. Nevertheless, the area of the blade edge is hardened to a higher degree than the blade back.

Wariha kitae: a blade edge of hard steel is forged onto soft steel.

Makuri kitae: blade combined of several steel types. Requires the highest forging skills.

Kombuse kitae: a v-shaped piece of steel forged onto an iron core.

For our tanto blade we used the maru kitae method: pieces of steel from the bloomery with different carbon contents were welded together and folded many times in order to achieve a relatively homogeneous structure. The blade edge was hardened to a higher degree than the back in order to get a break-resistant blade with a hard edge.

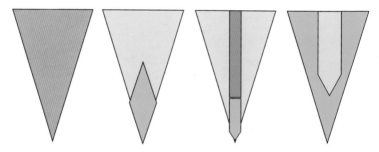

From left to right: maru kitae, wariha kitae, makuri kitae, kombuse kitae.

5.2 Forging the Blade

Because we forge steels with high carbon content, we have to consider that with increasing carbon content the steel reacts more sensitively to high temperatures. If the steel becomes too hot, coarse grains are created within the structure. This is not wanted, because the coarse grains impair the stability of the steel. If the steel is heated up to a glowing white color, sparks are created. The carbon burns up and the steel thus becomes unusable.

In practice this means that the steel during forging shouldn't be heated above a yellow orange color. As soon as the steel has cooled down to a dark red it has to be heated up again. However, for forging the following is valid: less is more. This means, the less often you have to heat up the steel again, the better it is for the steel. Thus uninterrupted and considered action is required.

The beginning: our billet from page 49 is first forged out lengthwise.

The forging fire is almost a science of its own: gas or coal, coke or charcoal. Each type of forging fire has its advantages and disadvantages. We have already described the differences in our book "Basic Knife Making" and thus we don't want to elaborate on this here.

The piece of steel which we use as raw material is first forged out to the appropriate length. A tip for this: a few drops of water on the anvil reduce the creation of cinder.

The tip is shaped. Forging the tip has the advantage that the structure of the steel follows the curve of the blade and thus the stability is enhanced. If the steel is just cut off in order to shape the tip, the structure is interrupted.

The tip is shaped with the hammer so that the structure of the steel follows the shape.

Here the tanto blade has already achieved its basic shape.

After forging, the blade is brought to its final shape at the belt grinder or by means of files. With a professional belt grinder the blade wedge can be shaped well. But be cautious: without training nothing works. The workpiece is quickly ruined because the abrasion happens very speedily. A simple belt grinder from the DIY store usually removes material slower. Accordingly, the work can be controlled better.

The tanto blade is further processed at the professional belt grinder.

Alternative belt grinder from the DIY-store: the star-shaped carbon explosions during grinding can be seen very well on this image.

The back is filed in the traditional shape with a central spine. Scratches from grinding and traces of files are removed with abrasive cloth. A sanding aid of wood is well suited for this. You proceed in several passes with ascending grit number (from coarse to fine). With each change of grit, the direction of polishing is changed as well which means you are working crosswise.

The back is filed evenly from both sides in order to create a spine in the center.

Abrasive cloth can be put on such a grinding aid.

The blade is already ground at the belt grinder.

The grinding marks are removed step by step with increasing grit size.

Important: the edge is not ground completely prior to hardening because it warps otherwise. You should leave about one millimeter of material and finish grinding only after hardening and annealing.

The final sharpening in no case ought to be done at a belt grinder or a quickly running grinding wheel which isn't cooled. A waterstone (see chapter 6.4) is ideal. Prior to using the waterstone, the bevel can be shaped with the diamond file. Prior to hardening, the hole in the tang ought to be drilled in which later on the retaining pin (mekugi) for the handle will rest. After hardening, drilling becomes strenuous.

After hardening: prior to sharpening with the waterstone, the blade edge is worked on with a diamond file. It takes off much more material.

AN EASY WAY FOR NEWCOMERS

For the beginner who wants to create a blade from a purchased piece of flat steel for a start there is the chance to buy material in a specialized shop. For a tanto, the following Japanese carbon steel types are suited best:
• white paper steel
• blue paper steel
Both steels are distinguished by their high purity (absence of un-wanted elements such as phosphorus, sulfur etc.) and high carbon content. They can be hardened to a high degree and blades of ex-treme sharpness can be created which are easy to re-sharpen, too. Laminated steel (suminagashi) from at least three layers of steel (usually two different types) is also suited well. Sometimes more than three layers are used.

No. 719615
Three Laminations Steel with
Hitachi White Paper Steel No.2

5.3 Heat Treatment

5.3.1 Basics

The heat treatment is extremely important for the later qualities of the blade. By means of annealing, the hardness can be controlled. The proper choice and temperature of the quenching agent is decisive for the hardness and a wrong decision can lead to the destruction of the blade.

Fact is: by wrong heat treatment good steel can be ruined while good heat treatment can even bring average steel up to highest performance.

Substantial literature exists about the complex processes inside the steel and the parameters which cause these processes. This is a science of its own. We want to confine ourselves to the basics and to teach the knowledge needed for what we want to do. Nevertheless, we can't get around some introductory sentences with respect to theory because you ought to understand what we are doing and why.

Basically, the blade ought to have a very sharp and long-lasting edge, but nevertheless should not break under stress or become permanently bent. To achieve these qualities there are two methods which we want to describe here: selective hardening and sandwich construction. During selective hardening, also called partial hardening, the edge area is hardened to a high degree while the back is made softer and thus more flexible. This technique we use for our tanto.

For the sandwich construction lateral layers of soft, non-hardenable steel are forged onto a core of highly hardenable carbon steel. The central layer, also called cutting layer, becomes hard and resistant to wear by hardening while the lateral layers stay elastic and thus support the cutting layer by their elasticity.

5.3.2 Selective Hardening

By means of this hardening method (also called differential hardening), which is typical for Japanese knives and swords, only the area of the cutting edge is hardened to a high degree; the back stays relatively soft and thus elastic. These qualities are created by different rates of cooling while quenching the blade. For this, the blade is covered with a coating of clay which is very thin at the edge and thicker in the back area. Within the thin area the steel cools down quickly and by this is hardened to a high degree. In the area of the thick clay coating the blade cools down slower, which in turn leads to lower hardness.

By this process different steel structures are created within the blade. The transition between these structures can be made more visible by polishing. This hardening line is called hamon in Japanese. The different schools teaching how to forge swords in the past developed their own patterns of hamon design, which means that a master's sword can be related to its creator by the pattern of its hamon.

The schools also used to keep secret the ingredients of the clay paste, the temperature of the quenching bath and the duration of staying in this bath. So the story goes that a smith while visiting the workshop of another bladesmith let his hand dip into the tub with the quenching water as if by accident. After this his host as quick as lightning chopped the hand off with his sword.

In general, Japanese smiths did not act gingerly in former times. To document the sharpness of a sword, the master marked on the tang which kind of cutting tests he had done with the sword. Besides mats from rice straw, corpses or prisoners sentenced to death were used as test objects. The accomplished cuts were described precisely so that the customer knew exactly which body parts the smith had hit successfully.

From a person sentenced to die in such a way the following is reported: After the manner of dying was announced to him, he complained that if he had known this before he would have swallowed a few stones in advance so that at least the sword would have suffered from this.

Back to the present from these horror stories and to the practical work on our tanto. First we need a suitable coating paste. As ingredients we used clay, flux and charcoal powder (about 80% clay, 20% charcoal, a small amount of welding powder).

With respect to the ingredients, there is a multitude of (secret) recipes from experts and those who think they are. In our opinion, it is only important that the application insulates well and sticks to the blade. The clay coating should not crumble when the blade is heated in the hardening furnace. The paste should not be too viscous either, in order to be easily distributed and to coat well.

In the area of the cutting edge the coating is done very thinly. The sides and the back are painted thickly to avoid too rapid cooling. The thick coating is partially drawn out to the area of the cutting edge to avoid stress caused by its different hardness.

When the layer of clay has dried well and doesn't crumble, the blade can be put into the furnace. Its time in the furnace should be until the blade has taken on an even, light cherry color. During heating you have to take care that the blade is heated up evenly over its entirety. Especially take care of the tip – it should not become too hot!

The ingredients of the paste: clay, flux and charcoal powder.

The paste is mixed. It should not be too solid, but not too fluid either.

The area of the blade edge is only covered with a thin layer.

Towards the back, which ought to cool down more slowly, the cover is much thicker.

How the cover is applied determines the later wave pattern of the hardening line (hamon).

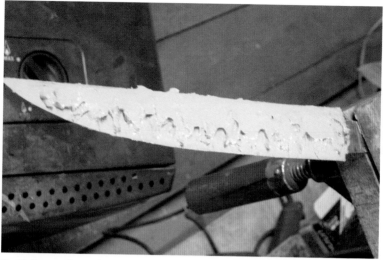

Partially we draw the wave pattern down into the edge area.

The clay layer has dried and the blade is waiting for the furnace.

After the blade has reached the hardening temperature of about 840°C (the corresponding color is light cherry red), it is put into the water bath with the edge first. It is best to slightly warm the water beforehand so that it is not icy cold. Tip: steel loses its magnetic properties at hardening temperature. A test with the magnet reveals whether the right temperature has been reached.

For the first time, it is recommended not to immediately harden the blade, but to try with a test piece of the same material. After several bitter experiences with quench cracking we started to do this as well.

In the furnace, the blade is evenly heated up to hardening temperature.

Prior to hardening our blade, hardening is first done with a test piece. After quenching it ought to be hard enough for a file to move across it without resistance.

The first attempt went wrong because the water was too cold: the test piece broke.

The moment of truth: the blade just prior to immersion in the water.

If the test piece develops cracks, then the water was too cold. We were successful with a temperature of about 45°C (bathtub temperature). No cracks were created and the blade was hard as glass. The file moved across it without resistance.

During quenching the blade warps upwards. For a sword, this is favorable because the cutting qualities of a blow are enhanced by this curve. The curve is created because the hard steel structure around the edge expands more than the soft structure of the blade's back.

During hardening usually some distortion is created. By careful adjustment on the anvil with the hammer (but only after annealing!), the blade can be straightened again.

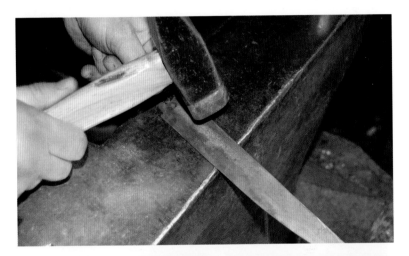

Straightening at the anvil: slight warp from hardening can be corrected after annealing.

5.3.3 Annealing and Sharpening

After hardening, the blade is annealed in order to bring it to useful hardness. Hereby the blade loses a bit of its hardness but also its brittleness. In a hardened, not annealed state, it would be too prone to cracks for a practical use. Under stress the blade edge would break like glass. Annealing is easiest at 200°C in the baking oven for about an hour. Afterwards the blade is cooled in lukewarm water.

Like the hocho, we sharpen the tanto blade on Japanese waterstones in the traditional manner. The process of sharpening, the waterstones and tests for sharpness are described in chapter 6.4.

TECHNICAL DATA OF OUR BLADE

steel: carbon steel 1.2%C
hardness: edge 62 HRC, back 48 HRC
blade length: 240 mm
blade width: 35 mm
blade thickness: max. 4.5 mm
weight: 150 g

So far, so good: our finished tanto blade.

The "ingredients" for mounting: stingray, ebony and a rectangular brass bar.

5.4 Assembling the Tanto

The production of a Japanese knife or sword traditionally rests in several hands. The individual worksteps were mainly distributed among the bladesmith, the polisher, the handle maker and the sheath maker. We did everything ourselves. For our project we chose the aikuchi form, which is an assembly without the guard (tsuba).

5.4.1 The Habaki

The habaki is a ferrule which is adapted to the end of the blade and covers its rear part and the front part of the tang. It ought to provide a firm fit within the sheath. Our habaki is made from solid brass. The drawing on the next page shows how the habaki rests on the blade. At first a piece of brass is cut to the needed length. The measure depends on the dimensions of the blade. We scribe the measurements of the blade onto the block of brass.

PROFILE OF THE HABAKI:

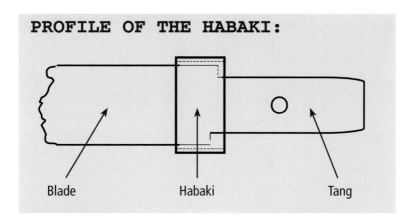

Blade   Habaki   Tang

The blade contour is transferred onto the brass block with a scriber.

For the opening we drill holes whose diameter is a bit smaller than the thickness of the blade. With a milling cutter we then remove the web (material left between the drilled holes). You can also cut through the web with a hacksaw and then refine the opening with a file.

We start with drilling a hole.

Several drill holes with smaller and smaller diameter are placed next to each other and the web between them is removed with a milling cutter.

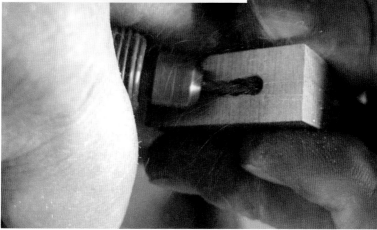

The saw blade is pushed through the opening and fixed in place.

This way we can saw out the contour inside the habaki.

In the end the final contour is shaped with a warding file. Here you should be very careful to achieve as small a gap as possible between blade and habaki.

Useful utensils in the workshop: small warding files.

With a small warding file ideally you can reach the end of the opening.

The brass piece is put onto the blade and carefully adjusted by means of a hammer.

With light blows, the gap towards the blade can be closed.

By well-dosed blows with the hammer on the anvil, the brass is cold-forged and hereby adapted to the blade contour.

For the gap in the habaki where the blade back is fitted in, we drill another hole with a diameter slightly smaller than the thickness of the blade's back. This gap is then filed to the right size with the warding file.

We drill another hole on the top edge of the habaki.

It is filed to form a notch for the blade back (see photo on p. 74, bottom).

Here the notch is to size.

The final shape is marked and created at the belt grinder. With the file you can add an elegant, inclined decorative filework such as we did.

With a felt pen we mark the shape on the habaki.

Superfluous material is taken off with the belt grinder.

A diagonal decorative grind adds optical value to our habaki.

Completed successfully: the finished habaki seen from the side and above.

ALTERNATIVE SOLUTION FOR THE HABAKI

Habaki can be made from different materials which also require different methods. As an alternative to the brass habaki we just made we show here how to create one from a piece of copper. As raw material we used a copper rod sized 3 x 30 mm.

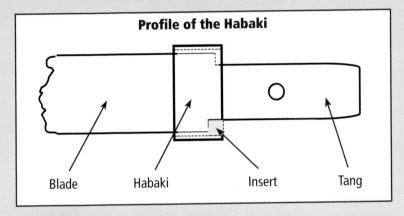

Profile of the Habaki

Blade   Habaki   Insert   Tang

A pretty example made from silver.

From the rod we first saw off a strip of the desired width for the habaki. In our case these are 15 mm. In the center, a groove is filed or milled to a depth of about two millimeters. The width of this groove is the same as the width of the blade back.

The strip is bent and cold-forged over a piece of flat steel. Afterwards the habaki is forged to shape on the blade. Copper becomes hard by forging in a cold state and then can only be shaped with a lot of effort. Thus it is necessary to soft-anneal the copper between the individual forging steps. By heating to annealing temperature and the following quenching in cold water the copper, contrary to steel, becomes soft again.

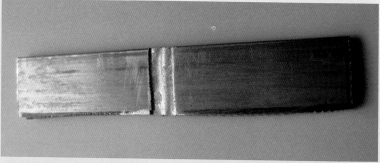

The copper strip is milled in the center (the width is the same as the thickness of the blade back).

Then the copper strip is slightly bent inwards.

As an auxiliary tool we use a piece of flat steel which is as thick as the blade back.

The material strength thus corresponds to the width of our filed groove.

The strip is cold-forged over the flat steel.

Afterwards the strip looks like this.

On the blade the habaki receives its final shape.

The shaped piece after cold-forging.

To provide a firm fit later and to prevent the habaki from slipping towards the blade, an insert is brazed on. For this we cut a suitable piece of copper to size. The habaki is put onto the blade and the insert is fitted in.

The habaki after soft-annealing.

The insert for the habaki is prepared.

The insert is fitted in so that the habaki can't slip on the blade later on.

It is brazed into the habaki (hard soldering with flame).

The habaki after brazing and reworking.

Brazing is done with silver solder (can be obtained at the DIY store). As a heat source we use a propane gas burner. Chamotte plates as a foundation and for shielding are a good aid.

As a match for our alternative habaki from copper, we now create a tsuba (guard), too. For this we chose a piece of flat brass about 2.0 mm in thickness. The measurements of the blade are transferred onto the flat metal and drill holes set for the opening. The opening is then shaped with the file. In case the opening of the tsuba doesn't fit, it can also be corrected by pushing out material with an ejector drift and then filing the opening to the exact size.

We set drill holes for the opening in the later tsuba and cut the web as before.

The brass sheet with the coarse opening.

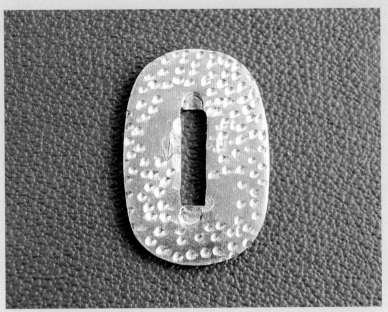

The tsuba seen from behind with the traces of pushed-out material. The outer contour was filed by us.

Habaki and tsuba in a mounted state: the finished alternative tanto.

5.4.2 Handle

For our handle we chose ebony. The piece of wood is cut into two halves and the space for the tang is carved out on the inside. With traditional Japanese handles, the cavity for the tang is not carved into both halves symmetrically, but with an offset. The reason for this is a practical one: if the seam between both handle halves is in the center, under load – for example during a blow – the largest force acts upon the weakest spot – the seam – and both halves can be blown apart. The drawing shows how the cut can be calculated in such a way that the tang lies in the massive part of the handle.

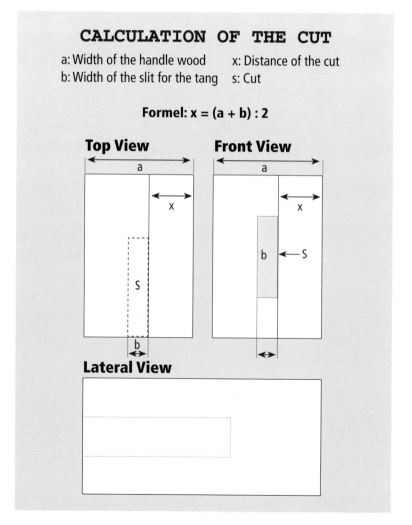

CALCULATION OF THE CUT

a: Width of the handle wood   x: Distance of the cut
b: Width of the slit for the tang   s: Cut

Formel: x = (a + b) : 2

Top View   **Front View**

Lateral View

The cavity for the tang should be carved out as exactly as possible with a sharp firmer chisel to provide a firm fit of the tang inside the handle.

Prior to glueing the two handle halves, on one side the hole for the retaining pin (mekugi) has to be drilled. For this the habaki has to be put onto the blade and the tang hole has to be marked on the handle scale. Then we are able to drill the hole into one of the handle halves and to glue it to the other half. Afterwards the drilling can be done on the other half with the already drilled hole in the first one as a lead.

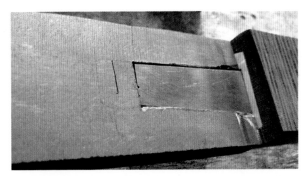

The tang is fitted into one half of the handle. The blade (on the right side of the photo) is inside the raw sheath.

The mekugi has been fitted in and only needs to be cut to the right length. The sheath is on the left.

The retaining pin of classic Japanese weapons is made of bamboo. It is produced from the dense outer area of a specially hardened piece of bamboo. For our project we used a piece of brass instead with a diameter of four millimeters.

It is important that the drill holes in handle and tang have a diameter of exactly four millimeters as well, because play has to be avoided. For a tanto, play would not be too tragic, but for a katana used during a cutting test a bad connection between handle and sword could have fatal effects. For a samurai warrior the mekugi was a kind of life insurance. In case it broke, the blade flew through the landscape while the warrior was left with the handle only. We covered the handle with stingray skin. To prevent the leather from protruding over the handle, material is removed from the area which has to be covered with leather to about the leather's thickness.

The area which has to be taken off is marked on the handle.

Material has been taken off around the handle in order to make room for covering it with stingray skin.

The retaining pin (mekugi) is kept at its initial length.

5.4.3 Menuki

Menuki are decorative elements with great symbolic force. They are put underneath the handle wrap and are held by it. The chosen motifs symbolize the virtues of the samurai and ought to bring luck to the person carrying the weapon. Favored motifs were dragons (symbol of luck), dragonflies (victorious insects which don't know retreat) and bamboo (faithfulness, unyieldingness).

For our tanto we chose a carp (koi) as a motif. The koi stands for perseverance and strength. In critical situations it stays calm. A Japanese proverb describes a calm person who doesn't start panicking in this way: like a carp on a chopping block. You can create menuki yourself, if you have the creative talent, but they are also commercially available.

Our (purchased) menuki depicts a koi.

5.4.4 Sheath

The sheaths of many tantos are elaborately made and often decorated with paintings, lacquer work (urushi) or inlays. The sheath's body usually is made from magnolia wood. But since we abstained from lacquering, we chose a piece of the same ebony from which the handle was made.

The sheath consists of two halves which were joined later. First, the blade's contour is marked on both parts. With the firmer chisel a fitting cavity is carved into the wood. The depth in principle corresponds to half the blade's thickness. In order to provide a firm fit inside the sheath a suitable cavity for the habaki is carved out as well.

The blade contour is worked into the wood by means of a firmer chisel.

The recess is adapted to the blade contour.

The fit for the habaki is worked in as well.

The habaki has to sit firmly inside the sheath.

Then both halves of the sheath are glued together with two-component adhesive.

Done: handle and sheath have received their final shape.

The result of a long process: our finished tanto from steel we produced ourselves.

HOCHO – THE JAPANESE KITCHEN KNIFE

Our first project is a kitchen knife of typical Japanese style. Prior to starting our work, we first explain what the special thing about it is.

6.1 Introduction

When in Japan with the disempowerment of the samurai in the year 1876 the production of swords was prohibited, the source of income for the swordsmiths was gone. Some smiths resorted to the production of kitchen knives. For this, they transferred the proven techniques and methods of sword production to the creation of knives.

Besides its functional shape, the Japanese kitchen knife excels because of its non-surpassed sharpness. The technical qualifications for the high sharpness are based on the used material as well as the structure and geometry of the blade.

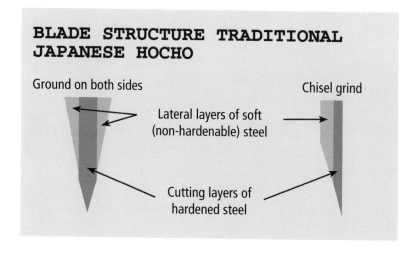

BLADE STRUCTURE TRADITIONAL JAPANESE HOCHO

Ground on both sides

Chisel grind

Lateral layers of soft (non-hardenable) steel

Cutting layers of hardened steel

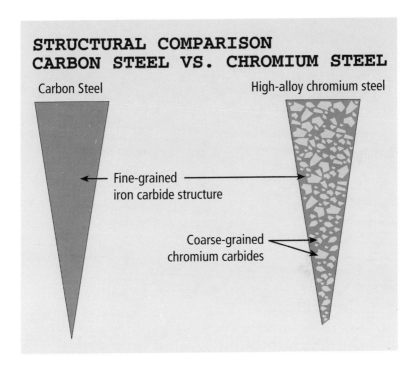

**STRUCTURAL COMPARISON
CARBON STEEL VS. CHROMIUM STEEL**

Carbon Steel

High-alloy chromium steel

Fine-grained
iron carbide structure

Coarse-grained
chromium carbides

The blade of a Japanese kitchen knife usually is forged from two or three main layers of steel. The cutting layer is made from carbon steel of high purity (white or blue paper steel*) with a high carbon content of about one percent. The lateral layers consist of soft steel or laminates of soft steels called suminagashi**. The soft lateral layers, which are welded to the cutting layer, support the hard cutting layer and provide the blade with the necessary flexibility.

The cutting layer of carbon steel can be ground very finely and becomes very hard, which has a positive effect on the durability of the blade edge.

---

* White paper steel (shirogame): carbon steel of high purity with 1.2% of carbon, high hardness, high edge retention, can be sharpened extremely, easy to resharpen, not stainless (steel for the cutting layer in blades made from several layers)

* Blue paper steel (aogami): similar to shirogame but with additions of 0.5% of chromium and 1% of tungsten, somewhat tougher than shirogame

** Suminagashi (Jap. "ink in the water"): The Japanese name is derived from the pattern of the steel, which looks like ink dissolving in water

OVERVIEW: THE MOST COMMON JAPANESE KITCHEN KNIVES

Santoku: Japanese "three virtues": the Japanese cook uses the knife for cutting fish, meat and vegetables, thus the name.

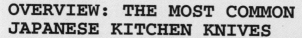

Usuba: Vegetable knife. The blade doesn't have a tip because this is unnecessary for processing vegetables.

Gyuto: Knife for fish and meat. The blade is slim and pointed, ideal for the preparation of fish and meat.

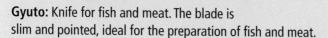

Ajikiri: Small knife for vegetables and lesser kitchen work. It is also used for weighing herbs.

Sashimi: Fish knife. The blade is long and pointed in the shape of a willow leaf or a katana.

Resharpening is no problem with carbon steel. In contrast to high-alloy stainless steel, the structure of carbon steel only consists of iron-carbon compounds (iron carbides), which are very small. Thus the steel has fine-grained structure.

Chromium in the steel, a guarantee for stainlessness, on the contrary, forms relatively large carbides. Thus it is technically impossible to grind an edge of chromium steel as finely as a blade edge of carbon steel.

With respect to their sharpness, Japanese kitchen knives are clearly superior to the most common European kitchen knives. Really sharp knives, besides their easier use, have the advantage that the food is cut in a gentle way and is not squeezed. Onions are cut without tears, because the substances which irritate the eyes stay inside the onion and are not squeezed out. The vitamins are also preserved because they don't get much into contact with the damaging oxygen of the surrounding air.

6.2 Forging the Hocho Blade

The task during the production of a hocho blade is to create a blade whose cutting edge excels in its high hardness and sharpness while at the same time being stable enough for daily use at the kitchen stove. Thus the concept is a blade with a cutting edge from a steel type with high carbon content and lateral layers of a much softer steel with less carbon.

As already mentioned, in the bloomery furnace pieces of steel with different carbon content accumulate, depending on their position within the furnace and the various parameters of the process. For the cutting layer, we have to sort out the parts with high carbon content. For the lateral layers the task is to find pieces with as low a carbon content as possible. To distinguish between them we use the spark test and also check them on the anvil with the hammer: hard pieces break like glass.

THIS IS THE WAY
OF A JAPANESE SMITH

The following photos of a Japanese master's forge were taken during a study trip of the author to various bladesmiths and manufacturers in Japan. They show the individual worksteps in the production of a hocho blade made by Master Shigefusa.

From raw material to the finished blade: stages in the process of creating a hocho-blade.

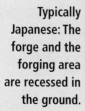

Typically Japanese: The forge and the forging area are recessed in the ground.

Master Shigefusa at the anvil: he strews flux onto the workpiece.

The layers of the blade are welded by means of a handheld hammer.

With a special scraper the surface of the blade is smoothed and brought into shape.

Our bloom is treated with the hammer; the steel pieces are uncovered and subsequently forged flat. They are ground to shape and stacked for welding.

Raw material: the raw bloom on the anvil.

Cut into pieces: an uncovered piece of steel.

Every single piece is forged flat on the anvil.

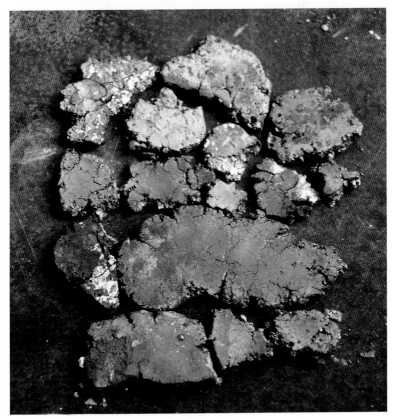

The flat-forged individual pieces prior to further processing.

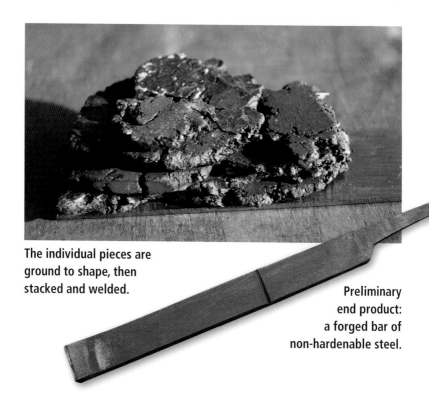

The individual pieces are
ground to shape, then
stacked and welded.

Preliminary
end product:
a forged bar of
non-hardenable steel.

We collected pieces of the loop steel which were soft and contained
only little carbon. The stacked pieces with low C-content were welded and forged out to form a bar.

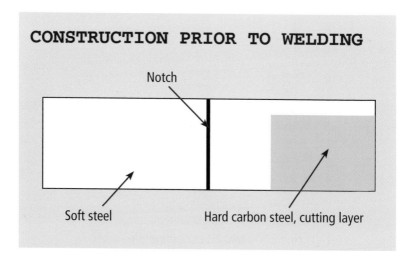

CONSTRUCTION PRIOR TO WELDING

Notch

Soft steel

Hard carbon steel, cutting layer

For the later cutting layer pieces with high carbon content were determined by means of tests. Those pieces were also welded and forged flat to a smaller piece. The insert is welded onto the basic material. Of course, this process is done in the forging fire. Prior to welding, flux has to be added. The drawing on the lower left schematically shows the structure prior to welding. The basic material is folded and welded to form a "sandwich".

The insert is ground to shape.

The insert for the core of hardenable carbon steel.

Flux is strewn onto the carrier.

The insert for the blade core is welded on prior to folding.

The steel is folded.

The whole thing seen from above: the hard insert is in the center.

The cutting layer is now firmly welded to the inside of the basic body. The billet can now be forged to shape on the anvil. Our hocho ought to receive the gyutu-shape. The forged blade is further shaped with files or at the belt grinder.

The gyuto-shape is forged out.

The blade is further treated at the belt grinder.

Here the blade has almost achieved its final shape.

Hardening and annealing we described in more detail for our second project, the tanto blade (chapter 5). In contrast to the tanto, no selective hardening has to be done with the hocho, since the stabilizing lateral layers stay soft because of their lack of carbon. Nevertheless, we covered the blade with a thin layer of a clay mixture in order to prevent strong scaling in the fire.

In order to make the course of the cutting layer visible, we slightly etched our blade. The layer is already visible across most of the blade. It will become even more distinct after final polishing.

THE TECHNICAL DATA OF OUR BLADE

blade length: 200 mm
blade width: 30 mm
blade thickness: max. 4 mm
weight: 150 g
hardness at the edge: 62 HRC

The blade after hardening.

The blade was slightly etched to make the cutting layer visible.

WAYS FOR NEWCOMERS

Since we don't expect all of our readers to immediately start or want to start with the steel production, we would like to show possibilities for creating a Japanese kitchen knife without steel produced by you in person.

Finished blade in Ajikiri-shape.

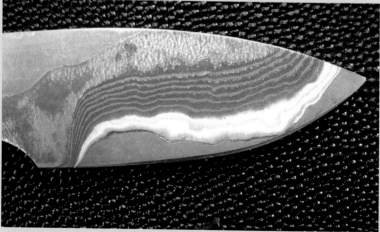

Prefabricated blade with sandwich construction: the hard cutting layer is in the center, on the outside are one layer of nickel and several layers of soft steel.

1. Buy a finished blade. This is the easiest way. Specialized shops offer good blades of Japanese production at prices between 30 and 100 euros.

2. Buy laminated flat steel and carve out the knife "off the solid", then (let it) harden and finish the knife. This solution gives you the chance to realize your own design.

3. Buy carbon steel (white paper steel, blue paper steel, 1060 etc.) and mild steel (St 37, i.e. material no. 1.0037), weld in the fire, forge the blade, create the knife and have the great feeling of using a self-made, one-of-a-kind knife in the kitchen. The image below shows how the billet for a blade with cutting core and lateral layers of soft steel (here: laminate) may look.

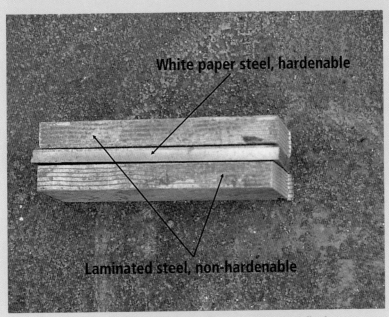

Compostion of a hocho-blade with hard cutting layer and flanks from laminate.

6.3 The Handle

The traditional Japanese handle consists of a single piece of magnolia wood with an oval cross section. Such handles are available pre-finished in specialized shops, which makes the construction of the knife much easier – in case you want to make it easier for yourself.

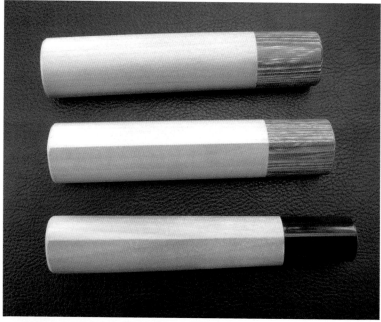

Pre-finished handles from bright magnolia wood with ferrules of precious bubinga wood and buffalo horn.

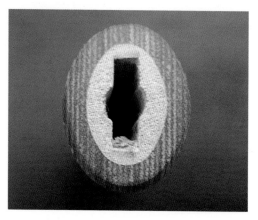

Here is a view of the drill hole for the tang.

The handle is attached in the following way: the blade is clamped into the vise with the tang facing upwards. Then two-component adhesive is filled into the drill hole of the handle which is then driven onto the tang with light hammer blows. The blade ought to be protected from damage by means of adhesive tape and a plastic hammer ought to be used for the task. Of course, the opening in the handle has to be wide enough for the tang. If it is too small, the wood will crack.

The Japanese often attach the handle by heating up the tang until it glows and then burning it into the handle while it is driven onto the tang. But using glue instead has the advantage that the handle opening is sealed and thus no moisture can accumulate there during use, which in turn means that no bacteria or fungi are able to settle there.

If you don't want to use a pre-finished handle, you can make it yourself. The charm of doing so lies in being able to choose an especially pretty piece of wood and the material for the ferrule as well.

The construction in principle is easy: you take a piece of wood and shape it according to your desire by means of rasping, whittling or turning. At the front end you file a step. Its outer diameter is identical with the inner diameter of the chosen ferrule. As ferrule, rod sections from non-ferrous metals, alloys such as brass or bronze, or stainless steel are well suited. The ferrule can also be made from a piece of buffalo horn, bone or other natural materials.

Our gyuto blade as finished knife with a handle of magnolia wood.

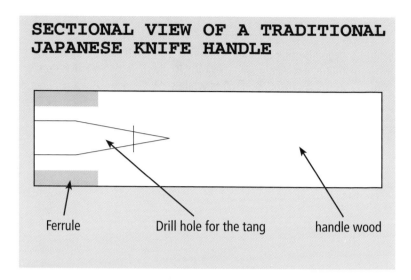

SECTIONAL VIEW OF A TRADITIONAL JAPANESE KNIFE HANDLE

Ferrule   Drill hole for the tang   handle wood

This handle was made from ebony and decorated with an opal.

Typical trait: asymmetrical cross-section of the handle with one corner at the side.

EUROPEAN HANDLE

An alternative to the traditional Japanese handle type is the European handle. This handle shape, gives the friends of Japanese blades a possibility to use their advantages while sticking to the familiar way of handling the knife by keeping the European handle shape.

6.4 Sharpening the Knife

Here we only want to describe the traditional way of sharpening with waterstones, because we believe this is the best way to create an optimal blade edge. Using a sharpening rod, as is common for European knives, is not appropriate for Japanese kitchen knives because the hardness of sharpening rods usually is lower than that of the cutting layer of a hocho. Besides that, Japanese kitchen knives which are ground on one side only are designed for a special sharpening method on waterstones.

In earlier times, natural stones from various Japanese quarries were used. Today these quarries are partially expended and the still available stones are relatively expensive. In the meantime, synthetically produced stones have also proved their worth. During production, various grinding particles such as metal oxides, carbides, diamond dust or semi-precious stones are imbedded into a basic mass (matrix). The manufacturer can precisely direct the properties of the sharpening stones by means of the type, hardness and number of grinding grains.

The grit size gives information about the fineness of the stone. The higher the grit size value, the finer the stone. Our recommendation for a beginner's set of stones:

coarse stone: grit size 220
sharpening: grit size 1,000
stropping: grit size 3,000
polishing: grit size 8,000

Very practical are combo stones with a layer each of grit size 1,000 and 3,000.

Japanese waterstones are available in many versions.

Prior to sharpening, it is necessary to water the stone. Japanese waterstones have open pores. They take in water like a sponge. The water is used as lubricant, coolant and for removing sharpening particles and rubbed-off metal parts. Because the stone's matrix is relatively soft, the stone is abraded during use. Thus new, fresh sharpening particles surface time and again.

The stone is clamped to best advantage into a fixture which was made for that purpose. It can also be put on a skid-proof base or on wet newspapers. Best is using the fixture, which can also be adapted to stones of every common size.

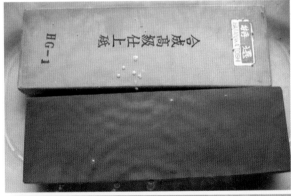

Prior to use, the stones have to be watered.

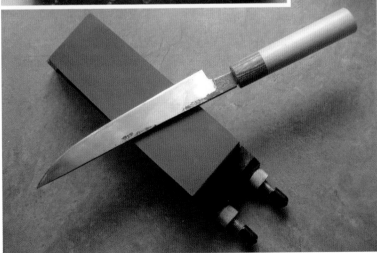

Very practical: a device for clamping the stone.

For sharpening, the blade is put flat onto the stone and is held by both hands at an angle of approximately 45°. Then the blade is tilted to the desired edge angle. For kitchen knives, half a thumb's width distance between blade back and surface of the stone is a good reference point.

Quite often the information about the angle is given as a precise number of degrees. We don't believe this information to be very helpful because the angle can't be kept to that precise number anyway. More important is to keep the chosen angle over the entire length of the blade edge. This can be done with a bit of training. To achieve a special feeling and view for this angle, we move back and forth along the entire length of the stone with the thumb on the blade and without pressure (otherwise the thumb becomes ground) a couple of times.

Simple aid: adjusting the angle by means of the thumb.

The edge at first is sharpened on one side.

During sharpening, the blade is guided with moderate pressure over the entire length of the stone forwards and back again. The pressure in both directions stays the same. The movement is straight. We don't move in the shape of eights or other figures on the stone. Keeping the angle would be more difficult by this and nothing would be gained. Information that you should only sharpen against the edge or in the direction of the edge is not based on any facts.

After a few passes you can see the dark abrasion of the stone. This is also a sign of where material is taken off the stone. Irregular abrasion shows that the sharpening process isn't being done evenly. A correction of your posture then becomes necessary. The stone shouldn't become too dry. Adding a few drops of water every now and then enhances the sharpening process.

Then the blade is turned around and sharpened on the other side.

Tip: You can control whether material is removed at the right spots during sharpening by marking the flanks of the blade with a felt pen. Then you will immediately see where the stone takes off material and you can correct the angle, if necessary.

After about 20 to 30 sharpening movements the knife is turned around. The right hand stays in the same position. Only the knife is turned around in your hand. After about another 20 to 30 repetitions we turn the knife in the hand again.

This process is repeated until the edge is ground completely. A good indicator for this is the creation of a burr. On the side opposite to the one we sharpened last a fine burr is created, which can be felt with a fingertip.

If you have ascertained that this burr extends over the entire length of the blade edge, you turn the blade once again, make one or two more draws and then change from the sharpening stone to the polishing and stropping stone. On this stone with its very fine grit size the burr is removed and the fine grooves from the previous sharpening process are polished away. With this, the blade receives its optimal sharpness. The right pressure during stropping and polishing is small, so don't press too hard!

Stropping on the stropping stone: the dark abraded material from the blade is clearly visible.

DRESSING THE STONE

If the stone shows signs of wear and is no longer planar, it should be dressed again. For this, dressing stones are available in specialized shops. But you can also take a flat slab of hard stone (granite), strew fine sand on it, mix it with a bit of water and strop the waterstone on it. For this it is put down flatly and is moved across the stone slab or stropping stone in the shape of the figure 8. By means of the abrasive tracks you can see very well whether the entire surface has been worked upon or whether dents are still left.

6.5 Sharpening Test

In order to test the sharpness of the blade edge, we take a sheet of paper in one hand, let it hang freely and then cut it apart with a single cut using the entire length of the edge. This lets us determine whether the blade still "plucks" at one spot or another.

Another well-proven test is the "tomato test". For this the blade is put on top of a tomato and guided across it without pressure. The hand only holds and guides the knife. The blade should sink into the tomato by its own weight alone.

If this succeeds, the knife is really sharp and well-suited for all tasks in the kitchen. Unfortunately, most kitchens are still equipped with a "tomato-squeezing tool" instead of sharp knives.

Easy to do: during the tomato test, the blade has to sink in by means of its own weight.

Paper test: the blade has to glide through the paper smoothly and without plucking.

CARE

Steels produced in the bloomery furnace are by nature not corrosion-resistant because they lack a sufficiently high chromium content. Nevertheless, as we already described under the topic of sharpening, this is no disadvantage. The lack of chromium is indeed favorable for the sharpness of the blade, since the blade edge can be ground finer without the coarse chromium carbides. The seeming deficiency of missing corrosion resistance can easily be balanced by a bit of carefulness and care.

Here are a few general tips for the care of the blades:

- Clean after use
- Always wipe dry
- Wipe off fingerprints
- Don't throw cooking knives into the drawer but keep them in the knife block
- Don't cut frozen food
- Distribute a drop of acid-free oil (e.g. camellia oil) finely over the blade every once in a while
- Don't keep the knives in a leather sheath for a longer period of time (tanning substances may attack the blade)
- Don't sharpen with a sharpening rod
- Don't clean using a dishwasher

APPENDIX

8.1 The Used Tools, Aids and Materials

Tools
- Bunsen burner
- dividers
- firmer chisel
- forge
- forging tools
- hacksaw
- hammer
- scriber
- spiral drill
- various files
- waterstones

Aids
- abrasive cloth
- borax
- charcoal
- clay
- flux
- spirit
- two-component adhesive

Other Things
- menuki
- pre-finished knife handle for Japanese kitchen knife

Materials
- ebony
- round brass material 4 mm stingray leather

8.2 Recommendations for Safety

Observing the following recommendations should go without saying, but doctors and nurses can tell you a thing or two about how careless some craftsmen are when dealing with their health.

- Follow the rules for working with machines.
- Don't wear loose clothing or jewelry while working with rotating machines
- Solvents and acids are to be used outdoors only. Wear protective gloves and goggles while working with them.
- Wear dust masks or respirators during all kinds of work where dust is created. The fine dust created while grinding can cause severe and lasting damage to your respiratory system.

- Wear protective goggles.
- Wear ear protection.
- While forging: always wear protective goggles, wear solid shoes (best: safety shoes) and solid clothing (not made of synthetic fibers!). Protect your hands by using thick gloves.
- While working on the tang and handle, cover the blade with adhesive tape.
- You absolutely have to follow the safety recommendations and rules for dealing with fluid gas!